MW01025910

TROLL

By Frid Ingulstad

Illustrations by Svein Solem

When human beings settled in the Northern Countries about ten thousand years ago, they soon discovered that it was already inhabited. Strange creatures had arrived before them. There were Elves and the subterranean folk who lived inside hills and knolls. There was the violin-playing *Fossegrimen* (pronounced fo-seh-greem-en) who dwelled beneath the rivers and waterfalls, and *Nøkken* (pronounced nuh-ken), the water sprite who ruled the black fathomless ponds in the middle of the woods.

But the most
terrible of them
all were the
gruesome trolls
who lived inside
the mountains.

With time, the humans accumulated valuable knowledge about the largest and most dangerous of all of nature's mysterious creatures. It was essential to know as much as possible about trolls if they were to have a chance of defending themselves in the event that they came in contact with one.

The trolls gave them answers to so many inexplicable questions: Where does evil come from? How could a huge boulder have been moved, unless a troll had thrown it? How could a rockslide appear, unless trolls had been throwing stones at each other? How could trolls disappear in daylight, unless they turned to stone when the sun shone on them?

Even though trolls were evil and dangerous, the humans discovered that they had one redeeming trait: they were stupid. They were so stupid that you almost felt sorry for them.

When you meet up with a troll, you may not be able to identify it right away. Even though some trolls are giants as big as a mountain or an evergreen tree, others are no larger than a human and are easily mistaken for them. These are perhaps the most dangerous kind. If you suspect you might be in the vicinity of one of them, the tail is the final proof.

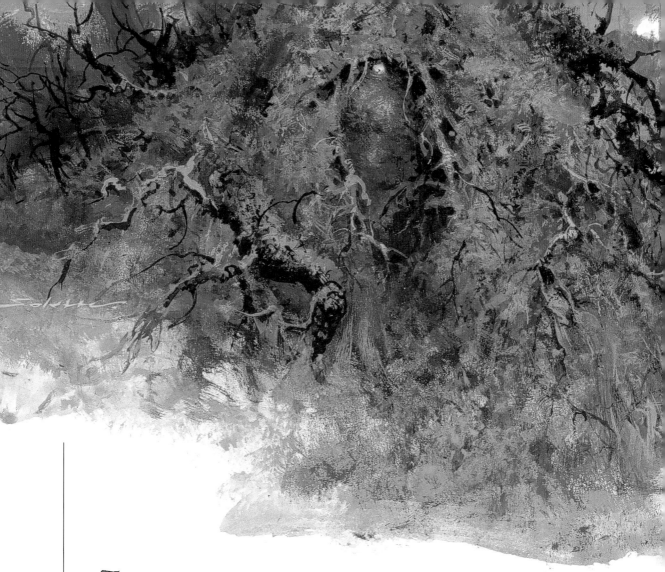

Trolls are ugly. The head is large compared to the rest of the body. The nose is crooked and full of warts, and sometimes as long as a broomstick. The mouth is large and full of yellow fangs. The eyes are small and squinting, though some trolls have only one eye in the middle of their forehead, and grass, heather and saplings grow on their crowns.

A very few of them are expert blacksmiths. Beautiful objects in iron and bronze made by trolls have been unearthed. The British Museum in London has a

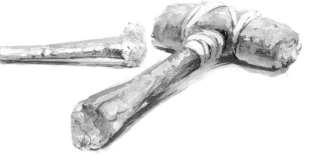

horn and a sword from the 12th century that were made by a troll.

About one thousand years ago Norway had two kings by the name of Olav, who ruled one after the other. They converted the country to Christianity and tried to get rid of both trolls and lesser gods. The law saying "It is forbidden to wake up trolls" came into being at that time. Trolls were considered enemies of the country, and the god Thor, you know the one with the hammer, was no longer allowed to "travel to the east to battle with trolls", and was himself considered to be a troll, and sometimes even the devil himself.

The trolls felt unjustly treated. They could not accept the fact that they were worse than humans. On the contrary, they felt that humans, despite their being so small and scrawny, managed to make much more trouble than trolls.

The word troll means "one who behaves fiercely". Trolls are terribly strong; they can throw boulders at each other, boulders that are as large as themselves. Boulders thrown by trolls can be found many places in Norway. In earlier times trolls used to throw boulders at churches, but they always missed because they have poor eyesight. The boulders lie beside the churches to this very day.

Large trolls can have as many as three heads, or even six or nine, in which case they are much easier to recognize. There are also trolls who carry their head under their arm, although no one quite knows why.

Trolls live in nature, on the inside of mountains and in the crests of ridges. Smaller trolls can also make their homes in caves, sheds and barns. Trolls sleep during the day and appear outdoors only after dusk. No troll likes daylight. When the sun shines on them, they either burst or turn to stone. All around Norway you can see petrified trolls, the Beisfjord troll, *Beisfjordgubben* in Narvik for instance, or the troll mountain peaks *Trolltindene* in Romsdalen, the Svolvær goat, *Svolværgeita* in Lofoten or the troll hag *Strandnesgygeren* in Vikedal.

Trolls can make themselves invisible or simply appear as dark shadows. In the same way that they can transform a human being, they can also transform themselves; into a prince for instance, or a goat, a black dog or a polar bear.

They can also change themselves into a tree trunk. A group of tourists experienced something of the kind a few years ago. It was a rainy day in the middle of August. The tourists had been walking for several hours and were beginning to feel weary. As they were about to enter a path, they discovered that it was blocked by a fallen tree trunk. One of the tourists took out his hunter's knife in order to cut off some of the branches. The tree trunk suddenly began to move. The rotting log creaked and groaned, the branches braced themselves on the ground, and in the next second the whole trunk started to draw itself up into a standing position, until a terrifying monster stood in front of the horrified tourists.

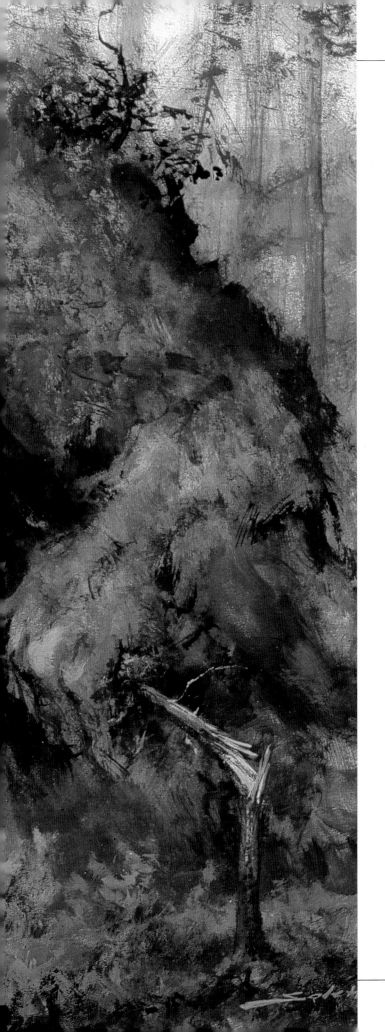

Another time a group of youths built a campfire on top of a hill in the woods. Suddenly a huge black dog unlike any other dog they had ever seen appeared. It came up to them and lay down beside the fire. In the same instant, the fire went out. The youths understood that this was pure sorcery and ran off as fast as they could. It seemed that they had made camp on top of a troll mound. The troll had been bothered and decided to scare them away.

But most often trolls are not satisfied with just scaring people. A long, long time ago there was a wedding on a large farming estate. A huge mountain troll arrived and wanted to taste the homemade beer, for trolls love beer. But no matter how much they gave him, he was not satisfied. At last they refused to give him any more. The troll trudged furiously off to the mountainside and started to chop it up so that the stones flew in every direction. They tumbled down the mountain and buried a large part of the valley. They lie there to this very day.

Something similar happened in another village. In this valley there were a whole row of large farms, and the farm owners there caroused and drank, quarreled and fought as they were used to doing. The troll sat inside the mountain and became more and more irritated over not being included in the fun. One day when there was more noise than usual down in the valley, he sent a boulder down the mountainside. But even though it crushed the first farm, the people continued to drink and quarrel as though nothing had happened. The troll became so infuriated that he fetched some really huge boulders from another valley, carried them to the top of the mountain and sent them toppling down so that they filled the entire valley. All of the farmhouses were crushed, and everything but a rooster was killed. For seven years the rooster climbed the rock-strewn slope and crowed at dawn as a reminder of what had occurred and as a warning to take trolls' threats seriously.

Trolls are egocentric. They rarely think of others, but can make an agreement with humans or with other trolls if there is something in it for them. They love to kidnap beautiful women, especially princesses.

They are always fighting with each other. Only when they are confronted with a common enemy, can they be friends. They can be devilish and laugh until their sides ache when they have managed to trick someone or if another troll makes a fool of himself. Sometimes they laugh until they burst.

Only on rare occasions can a troll do a favor for a human, for there are a few of them that are basically good. An old man who lived alone had lost count of the days as Christmas drew near. He had no idea that it was already the day before Christmas Eve. Then a voice shouted from the mountain:

- One night, one day, then count no more
For Christmas Eve will be at your door.

A young boy once experienced something both frightening and unexpected. The boy did not like being at home, but preferred to walk in the mountains, hunting the whole day long. He went off every day no matter how much his parents scolded. Once when he had walked very far, and further than far, he caught sight of something that shone in the distance. He followed the lights and discovered that the *Hulder* (pronounced: hooldare) people were living there. He then heard one old crony say to another one:

– Can I borrow that big pot of yours?
– What are you going to do with it? the other one asked curiously.
– I plan to cook that disobedient boy who never wants to stay at home.

The boy became frightened and ran off but suddenly he heard a thundering and roaring behind him, and when he looked he saw a frightful, giant troll coming after him. He dashed down the slope with the troll behind him, came to the edge of a large lake, but the ice was so slippery that he couldn't walk across it. Just then another troll shouted to him from a nearby ridge:

- Take off your shoes, then he won't be able to catch you! The boy did as the troll said, reached the other side safely, and from that day forward he stayed at home.

Trolls are thieving creatures as well. When people cannot find what they are looking for, or when a farmer cannot explain how the potato cellar could be empty so soon, you can be sure a troll is the culprit. They change themselves into mice or rats, hide under floorboards and follow what the humans are doing. Sometimes they borrow things, for instance a pair of scissors, car keys or a pair of glasses, but then they become so annoyed because they don't know what the objects are used for that they fling them in disgust and that's how they end up in the wrong place.

No one knows how old a troll is, but we do know that they can become unbelievably old. A young troll can have seen three oak forests grow up and then disintegrate, while an old troll can have seen it happen as many as seven times. Inside a mountain in the south of the country lives a mountain troll that was born in the age of the Vikings.

He has shrunken to such an extent that he sits inside a horn that hangs on the wall. His son sits by the hearth and fries bacon fat when he is not sleeping. He is so ancient that he looks like a dried out tree stump. His head quivers back and forth, and his hand shakes so much that most of the bacon fat falls into the flames. Even his son is old, and yet all three of them are frightfully strong.

Troll language resembles the dialect that people speak in the areas where trolls live. Trolls express themselves ambiguously, especially when they are about to perform some sinister act. For instance they say "throw blueberries" when they mean to shoot, "large dog" instead of bear, and "blood of a Christian" means humans.

The only way a human can escape a troll alive – aside from fooling it – is to hold up a piece of steel or a cross, or to recite a passage from the Scriptures. A courageous parish clerk once stole into a troll cave and poured sacred wine into the food. The trolls became so confused that they beat each other to death. If you meet a troll by a field you should run across the field at a right angle to the ploughed furrows. Your tracks will form a cross and the troll won't dare to follow you.

Trolls are so easy to fool that even small children can deceive them. A young boy that was overtaken by a mountain troll that bellowed at him in the woods, took a cake of cheese out of his sack, squeezed it so that the whey squirted in every direction and shouted to the troll: – If you don't keep quiet I'll squeeze you just like I'm squeezing the water out of this white stone!

– No, please, spare me! exclaimed the troll with horror.

On the same day the boy tricked the troll into an eating contest with him. He had secretly hung his sack under his shirt and poured more porridge into that than into his stomach. When the bag was full, he took out his hunting knife and slashed a hole in it so that the porridge spilled out. – Do what I did, he said to the troll, – if you cut a hole in your stomach you can eat as much as you please. The troll did as he was told, and it cost him his life.

Another boy was walking in the woods with his little brother one day when they met a three-headed troll with only one eye. – Curses, it stinks of Christian blood here, roared the troll. The boy took his axe and hit the troll in the heel so that it threw its head in pain. The eye popped out and fell down in between the heather, and the boy was quick to pick it up.
– Oh, please give me my eye back and you shall have all the gold and silver I have in my mountain, begged the troll.

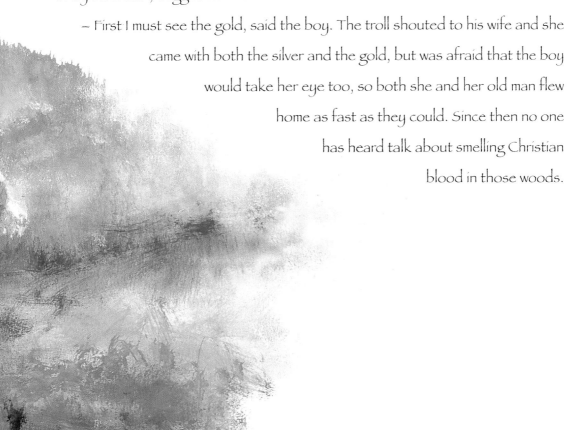

– First I must see the gold, said the boy. The troll shouted to his wife and she came with both the silver and the gold, but was afraid that the boy would take her eye too, so both she and her old man flew home as fast as they could. Since then no one has heard talk about smelling Christian blood in those woods.

Most trolls are dumb. We have many examples of that. One winter day a giant troll stood brooding on the top of a mountain. He was feeling lonely and unhappy. He had no one to fight with, no one to quarrel with, no one to eat up, and no one to get annoyed at. Then he suddenly caught sight of a beautiful troll girl on the mountain on the other side of the lake. Her nose reached almost down to her knees, she was big-bottomed, flat chested and bow legged. He became so excited that he jumped on his sled and coasted full speed down the slope. The troll girl saw him and took off down her mountain on skis. Once arrived by the water they remained standing on either side of the lake and scratched their heads both thoroughly and well trying to figure out how to cross it. Neither of them understood that it was possible to walk around it. Suddenly the sun appeared and they both turned to stone. They still stand there to this very day, looking at each other and waiting for the lake to freeze solid in a new ice age or to evaporate in the heat of a desert.

The most disgusting thing a troll can imagine is when humans do good deeds, have heroic dispositions, or are unusually daring. For it is precisely this kind of hero that succeeds in eliminating trolls; either with the help of raw strength, courage and suppleness, by stabbing the troll under the sole of its foot, cutting its tail or simply cutting off all of its heads.

On the other hand, some trolls are impossible to do away with. These are the ones who have concealed their hearts miles away in another country. The Svånås Devil, *Svånåstyggen*, for instance, has its heart concealed in a dragon in a country in the East. Inside the dragon is a rabbit, inside the rabbit is a duck, inside the duck is an egg, and inside the egg lies his heart.

One of the greatest dangers involved in meeting a troll is being bewitched. Anyone can fall under their spell and be drawn into the mountain, but women who have recently given birth are more susceptible than others. The only method for keeping safe is to wear an article of clothing belonging to your husband. This method worked for a young mother a few years ago. Just as she passed through the entrance to a troll mountain, she heard a booming voice cry from inside the mountain:

– Get her! Get her!

– I can't. She's wearing her husband's shirt, answered the other.

Of those that are caught, some are held prisoner for only a few minutes or hours, while others never return. Ringing a church bell can rescue someone under the spell of a troll. Until a few years ago, you could find bells for just this purpose many places in Norway. They were attached to a band of braided twigs that fit perfectly around a wrist.

If it is too late and you are already under a spell, the following rules apply:

✠ Do not reveal your name to the trolls.

✠ Do not drink or eat anything the trolls offer you.

✠ Say a prayer or recite a verse from a hymn. In this case the trolls will first get agitated, but soon they will lose all their strength and forget to guard the gate.

Living in a country with so many trolls is fraught with other dangers as well. You can risk having your child exchanged for a troll child! Shiny steel, a psalm book or garlic in the house diminishes the risk, but the damage can already have been done. Parents don't notice anything at once, but as time passes they begin to suspect that the child is a changeling. The child eats them out of house and home, its head swells and hair grows inside its ears. A troll child can give itself away by climbing out of the cradle, creeping over to the table and eating up all the food.

In order to help people distinguish between inhabited and uninhabited mountains, troll mountains, troll waterfalls or troll mounds are drawn in on the map. It is worth your while to study it well before setting off on a trip. Most dangerous of all is to go hiking in the mountains when there is fog. It is very easy to mistake a troll for a huge boulder. Dovre is the mountain range in northern Europe most abundant in trolls. Stones painted with a red T – red for danger, T for troll – mark all of the dangerous mountain areas.

Some trolls are exceptions. Take the *Ekeberg Troll* for instance, the only troll in the world that lives in a capital city. He shuffles mournfully along the crest of Ekebergåsen in Oslo with bowed head, running eyes, and wads of moss in his ears and holding his nose because of the exhaust and noise from the traffic. During the Middle Ages, people were deathly afraid of him. When the noise of thunder and booming came from inside the hill, they went to bed at night quaking with fear.

In Trondheim it was the *Ladehammer troll* who built the spire on the Cathedral of Nidaros. The king had promised his own life as a reward to whoever succeeded in building the church spire. The Ladehammer troll offered to do it without payment if the king could guess his name. By the time the tower was finished, the king had still not been able to guess his name. One day while he was sailing on the fjord below Ladehammer mountain, he suddenly heard a troll woman trying to hush a screaming child by saying that he would get the king's head to play with when Tvester came home. Upon hearing this, the king hurried back to the church and shouted up to the troll who was putting the last touches on the spire:
– Tvester! You've built the tower too far westward!

When the troll heard the king call out his name, he fell from the tower and nearly killed himself. Fortunately, the spire remained intact!

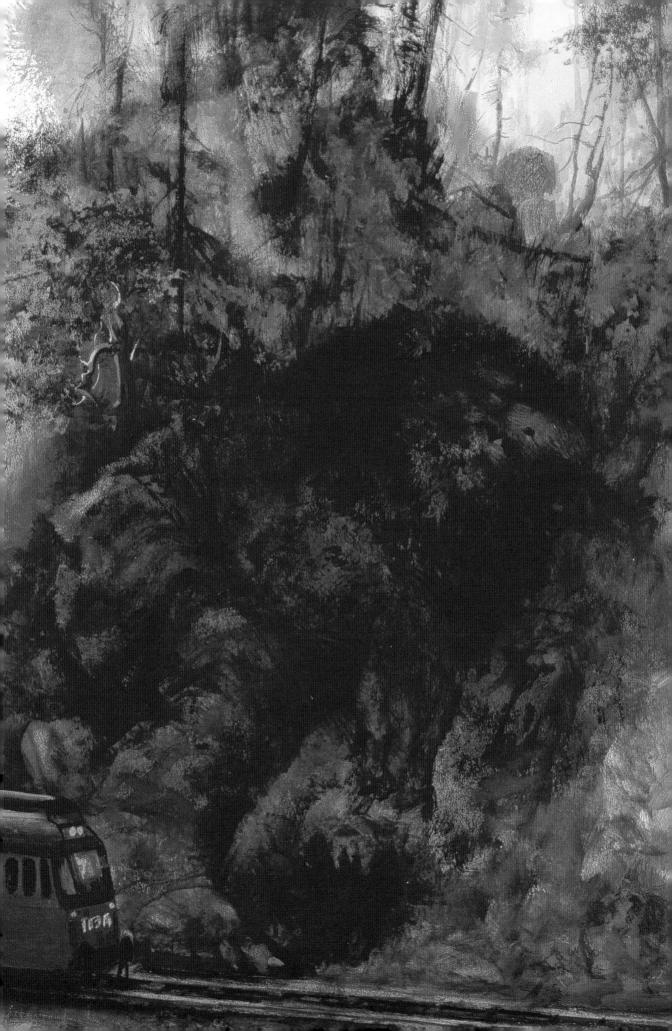

In the old days the kings from these parts used to be able to turn trolls into stone.

Once when Olav the Pious came riding on his horse along a steep slope leading to

a narrow valley, a troll hag came flying out of the mountain and shouted at him:

– Tell me, man with the beard so red and stiff: Why do you ride so close to my cliff?

But Olav was not so easily frightened so he shouted back at her:

– Stand as stone in that same spot

And harm anyone more you shall not.

And so it was. You can still see the petrified troll hag standing there in the mountain.

They have finally been given permission to set up a sign cautioning against trolls by the tourist spot called *Trollstigen* (Troll ladder). The sign is in defiance of the Vienna Convention as well as traffic regulations, but the Commissioner of Highways made an exception because this was 'a very special case', as it was stated. If too many tourists disappeared without a trace at Trollstigen, it would scare tourists away from Norway.

The following advice can also be given:

✠ Keep your eyes peeled around sundown and be on the lookout for fresh troll tracks.

✠ Study closely all dark shadows, bowed evergreens, and mountain peaks or hills that resemble a troll.

✠ Watch out for people who guzzle unusually large quantities of beer or who swear more than usual. They could be trolls disguised as humans.

✠ Be careful when you meet polar bears, black dogs, princes or goats. They could be trolls in disguise.

✠ Make a detour around a rotting tree stump. It could be a troll trying to fool you.

© Egmont Bøker Fredhøi AS - SFG
N - 0055 Oslo
www.touristbooks.com

Distributed in USA by:
Skandisk Inc.
6667 West Old Shakopee Road
Suite # 109 Bloomington
MN 55438-2622 USA

Author:
Frid ingulstad

Illustrations:
Svein Solem

Translation:
Francesca M. Nichols

Editor:
Trude Solheim

Design:
Sissel Holt Boniface

Printed at Nørhaven AS, 2000

ISBN: 82-04-06956-1

Also available:

DESTINATIONS COLLECTION

The Best of Norway

Languages:
Norwegian
English
German
French
Spanish
Italian
Dutch
Russian
Portuguese
Japanese
Chinese
Korean
Finnish

CLASSIC COLLECTION

Norway – incl. CD

Languages:
Norwegian
English
German
French
Spanish
Italian
Japanese
Russian

A Taste of Norway

Languages:
Norwegian
English
German
French

Th. Kittelsen: Trolls

Languages:
Norwegian
English
German
French
Spanish
Italian
Japanese
Dutch

HISTORY REVISITED

The Vikings

Languages:
Norwegian
English
German
French
Spanish
Japanese
Italian
Dutch
Swedish
Danish
Icelandic
Russian

Viking Cookbook

Languages:
Norwegian
English
German
French
Spanish
Danish

CHILDREN'S COLLECTION

Magnus Viking

Languages:
Norwegian
English
German
French
Spanish
Danish

Elgar

Languages:
Norwegian
English
German
French
Spanish

The Little Troll

Languages:
Norwegian
English
German
French
Spanish
Italian
Japanese
Dutch
Swedish

If your local retailer does not stock our titles, please visit our web site: www.touristbooks.com